COOKIN' WITH
FRIENDS
140 CHARACTERS OR LESS

One man's passion of cooking, friends, and making memories

Mark T. Carboni

First Edition 2013

First printing 2013
Printed in the United States

ISBN 978-0-9837469-1-1

DEDICATION

In the winter of 2013, I lost my mother from a massive heart attack. The pain has been like no other I have experienced before, and I learned that letting go is the hardest thing to do. We shared an enthusiasm for life, cooking, and friends; I am my mother's son and very proud to be that. I hear the echoes in my head of her voice, sharing how proud I have made her. I dedicate this book to her memory and to honor her guidance, wisdom, and love. She made every dinner or gathering into a moment of making lifetime memories that I now carry with me like a scrapbook in my mind. To friends and family...
I love you, Mom.

Proof that I have always loved cake!

ACKNOWLEDGEMENTS

My journey has been made possible because I have the most amazing circle of friends. I would like to say thank you to Tim Jones for enduring this journey step by step. He is truly amazing! Four years later I still feel the same as I did on day one. Jennifer Bosk and Barb Richards for being my second family. Laughter is fat-free, luckily, because we indulge in this behavior often. To one of the most creative and inspiring friends, Joel Gabbard, I thank you for always being there when I need an ear. Annette Roy, Cindy Reichwage, and Becky Rowan for being life long friends that have been by my side and in front of me to help lead the way. Deborah Rhoades, Aaron Rothgeb, and Susan Morgan for inspiring me in the kitchen. Liz Schatzlein who has a heart of gold and truly the closest person to a saint that I know.

ChristmaSITdown was a casual wine tasting celebration. Everyone had a bottle of wine and an appetizer sitting on the floor next to them. Each person would pass the food and the wine for a fun holiday celebration!

Life long friends: Becky Rowan and Mark Carboni

Wine tasting event

PREFACE

I find myself most at ease hosting a party, planning an event, or hanging with friends. Since the advent of our Cookin' with Carbo Facebook page, the interaction has been staggering. Over 1.4 million friends have found themselves in front of their mobile devices, laptop or desktop computers, checking out our page and sharing thoughts and tips.

I knew that my next cookbook needed to feel comfortable, warm, and welcoming to all of my media friends. I have invited these people from around the world to be a part of our volume 2 of Cookin' with Carbo. A social interaction cookbook has been born.

Our "pop-up" boxes are bubbling over with great cooking tips, regional and cultural information, and home spun anecdotes. We all have something unique and special to share from our knowledge, love, and compassion of cooking.

I do want to hear from you. Do please find us on the web at www.facebook.com/carbocooks and direct email at cookinwithcarbo@me.com

Mark T. Carboni is a classically trained home-chef. When he says classically trained, he means by the hands-on experience of his Italian grandmother.

He prepares simple, yet elegant food selections for any occasion.

My grandmother, Loraine Mozzone

FOREWARD

I am the unlikeliest person ever to write a foreword for a cookbook. Twenty-five years ago, a friend signed me up for private cooking classes as a wedding gift. My husband and I had to replace the stove top twice during the first year of our marriage, from various culinary disasters I caused. Although I've gotten a little better through the years, I am still pretty much of a lost soul when it comes to food preparation. Even our dog prefers her bagged dry kibble to much of my cooking. So why am I writing this? While I may not know a roux from a radish, there is something I do know about — the goodness that is Mark Carboni.

This is Mark's second cookbook, a follow-up to his phenomenally successful first effort, "Cookin' with Carbo." This time, Mark has chosen a friends and family theme, and that is only appropriate. Mark Carboni has never met a stranger. Put him in a room with twenty people he's never met, and he'll be on a first-name basis with fifteen of them within 30 minutes. People are naturally drawn to this warm, approachable man, and he enjoys lavishing his time and attention on those he cares about. People express their love for others in many ways; Mark shows it through the magic in his kitchen. If you have been lucky enough to be on the receiving end of one of his meals, you know his culinary skill goes beyond impeccable presentation and taste. You feel he is presenting you with a gift, a gift that he has poured all his heart and soul into, prepared just for you. Cooking equals caring to Mark Carboni, and he cares a lot.

When my father died unexpectedly last year, Mark was one of the first people to come to my side — and he never left. He patiently listened to me work through my grief, and after the memorial service he opened his home to my family and friends with a feast fit for royalty.

He provided exactly what was needed at that moment — a strong shoulder, a warm hearth, and a loving meal. While I can never repay him for his kindness, I can let the world know what a special person he is.

With Mark, it isn't just about the food. The food is an expression of his passion for life and his enjoyment of his friends and family. It's the message behind the meal that counts. Mark never slaves over a stove, because it's not work. He loves every minute he is creating something special for a luncheon or a dinner. And the only thing he loves more, is watching you devour it. If you walk away filled and happy, with an emphasis on the happy part, he feels he has succeeded.

You don't need to be a trained chef to follow one of Mark's recipes, and I sincerely thank him for that! Whether you really know your way around a kitchen, or need a GPS device to get from the refrigerator to the stove, this book makes it possible to whip up a wonderful meal. Life is complicated enough, and Mark Carboni makes cooking simple and fun. In his world, cooking and dining are celebrations of the joy he finds and shares in every single day.

Mark is an enormously talented cook. He is an even better friend. Enjoy!

Liz Schatzlein
Nashville, Tennessee

Jennifer Bosk, Barb Richards and Carbo sitting in the lawn for a series of concerts at the Country Music Associations Festival.

CONTENTS

Tiffany Blue table all set!

Sandy Thomson and
Tim Jones at Carbonanza,
the country holiday party
theme, where we had
animals for photo
opportunities and petting.

THOUGHTS ON MY PARTIES

You know, over the years I have had some great social gatherings. One that stands out was Carbonanza! Torn from the pages of a great western, we had live animals, like donkeys and sheep, in the garage for photo opportunities. We had a 30 foot food buffet of all the country comfort foods imaginable. An open bar and over 200 people in attendance, it became one of the largest gatherings I have ever held.

I love finding ways to gather a group of friends together. Coming up with a food theme begins the brainstorming for what I hope will be a night packed with memories. One dinner party that was a high point was my "Dinner at Tiffany's." I combined a multi-course dinner on white plates. The tablecloth was Tiffany blue with a large white bow on the table (just like a Tiffany gift box). It was such a pretty table.

Every year, I have a tradition called Thanksgathering. It began as a way to gather friends together that did not have plans for Thanksgiving. I would make the turkey and everyone would bring a side. On one of the first gatherings, everyone brought pie! We had turkey and pie. Everyone said they brought a pie because they knew I loved pie… and so it was, a pie harvest meal. Today, Thanksgathering means five turkeys being made for about forty friends!

One of the most talked about parties was a wine tasting event. Picture this: I removed all of the furniture from my living room. I placed glass blocks with a twelve-by-twelve inch mirror on top. I placed a bottle of wine in front of each one, with fresh cut flowers and candles between each spot. Cushions and pillows were placed on the floor for sitting. We passed appetizers and wine with great chill music and conversation all night long. You know, I think we try so hard to make a perfect event for people. What I find out is if you just make your guests comfortable and have something to do or talk about, well then they are all set.

THE FRIENDSHIP STARTER: A DRINK STATION

Set up a drink station for your party that gets friends talking and gives them, simply, something to do. I know you will think of your favorite cocktails and drinks to add to your station, but here is a starter.

This year, I did a few container gardens with mostly herbs. I am realizing fresh herbs make everything you cook taste better and fresher. The most bountiful herb this year has been my mint. Have it on your deck or patio right by the door so you get a fresh scent every time the door opens or you breeze by.

The scent of mint is so calming, and when coupled with fresh berries or a glass of iced tea, it is refreshing. I wanted to share a way that I can keep some fresh mint simple syrup on hand, for up to a month in the refrigerator. I would recommend the syrup be an additive to your iced tea, lemonade, or our blueberry mojito recipe.

Man your drink station with simple syrup, berries, lemons, limes, lemonade, iced tea, and of course ice. Set out our blueberry mojito recipe with suggestions for other mixes, and even let your guests get creative and make their own concoction that you might just name after them. You can even have bottles of your mint simple syrup to go after the party is over.

Cindy Reichwage and Carbo at the christening of the new kitchen, where we had over 30 foot of counter space with food and beverage for everyone to enjoy

Tim Jones, Carbo and Sue Fyfe at Doughvember! The annual cooking baking event where friends gather and bake off cookies and share. Three sessions of baking takes place on this annual November Saturday ritual.

MINT SIMPLE SYRUP

INGREDIENTS

1 cup sugar

1 cup water

30-40 leaves of mint, chopped

DIRECTIONS

In a saucepan, over medium heat, add all ingredients and stir consistently. Just before it comes to a boil, remove and allow to sit for 10 additional minutes. Strain the mint and place into refrigerator, covered, until ready to use.

This will make about 8 ounces of syrup. A few tablespoons will be all you will need in your beverage.

THE FRIENDLY BLUEBERRY MOJITO

INGREDIENTS

1 cup fresh blueberries, plus extra for garnish

16 ounces Sprite or 7 UP

10 fresh mint leaves

½ teaspoon brown sugar

Juice of **2** limes

Ice

Mint simple syrup to taste

DIRECTIONS

In a food processor or blender, puree blueberries until smooth. Set aside.

Add mint leaves and the brown sugar to each glass. Get your friends to help you muddle the mint with the end of the spoon or muddler. Squish those mint leaves and sugar. Add the lime juice, soda, and pureed blueberries and stir. Add mint simple syrup to taste. Garnish with a lime wedge, extra blueberries, and a sprig of mint.

Will make 4 small glasses.

INTRO TO SWEET TREATS

 **Mark T. Carboni** Cotton candy or candy corn? Your choice...

 **Janice Baum** Candy corn mixed with peanuts.

 **Lisa Thompson** Candy corn!! With salted peanuts.

 **Deidra Center Gulley** Both...one in the summer and the other fall.

 **Becky Hull** Candy corn, peanuts, and plain M&Ms....great fall mix snack for parties!!! (Use the fall colored M&Ms)

 **Melissa Cordial Schenkel** Cotton candy all the way

 Michelle Beary Candy corn is banned in France due to the ingredients that it contains.... My husband is not a happy man! Cotton candy isn't!

 **Karen Zonis Belcher** I love candy corn.

 **Jori Katras Stiffarm** Candy corn – the chocolate kind

 **Lisa Taylor-Vences** Cotton candy – blue pleez!

ANNE COCHRAN'S GRANDMOTHER'S BEST COOKIES: SAND TARTS

I love live music performances. I have attended hundreds of concerts. Over the years I have become a huge follower of Jim Brickman and his amazing vocalist Anne Cochran. In all, I have attended twenty performances. I promise to Anne I am not a stalker but a strong avid fan.

For my 40th birthday, Anne performed a private show with 40 of my dearest friends and family. Her angelic voice, her humor, and originality made the evening magical. An evening that I shall never forget and hopefully my friends enjoyed as well.

My mother became her second biggest fan, following me, of course. My mom loved her song "Colour Everywhere," and my favorite is her original penned single "Make it Right."

I find that a song can make a bad moment turn good, and whatever song I play seems to reflect my mood at the moment. I find that Anne's voice is one that brings me great joy and lightens my spirit, so I have a feeling these cookies will do that too. Her contribution to my cookbook not only makes me beam from ear to ear, I am certain my mother, if she was here, would be just as overjoyed as I am.

INGREDIENTS

1 cup butter (room temperature)

½ cup powdered sugar

2¼ cup sifted cake flour

¼ teaspoon salt

1 teaspoon vanilla

6 ounces chocolate chips

DIRECTIONS

Mix sugar with butter. Add vanilla, salt, flour (little by little), and nuts. Hand mix and refrigerate over night.

Roll into balls, flatten, and place ½" apart from each other. Place in a 325 degree oven for 15 minutes.

Cool a bit, and then roll in powdered sugar.

Anne Cochran Our memories include annual holiday baking sessions with my grandmother, my mom, and y sister. My mom worked with Jim Brickman's mom, Sally, at CWRU. She was also driven to work every morning, by Sally. In her appreciation, my mother would bake these cookies for Sally and her boys, every holiday season. To Jim, my mother's handwriting looked like "Sand Toots," not "Sand Tarts," so these cookies now baked every year, by my sister Wendy, for the holiday tour's cast and crew, are forever referred to as "Sand Toots."

Anne Cochran is a singer-songwriter from Cleveland, Ohio. She is best known as the lead touring vocalist for pianist and songwriter Jim Brickman, with whom she shared the top 5 Adult Contemporary hit single "After All These Years" in 1998. www.annecochran.com

LIME COOKIES

Got to tell you, the first batch must have been bad, because they were gone within seconds. The second batch I made I was certain to get one! They are yummy. If you are doing a tea or shower-brunch, these will be a hit.

INGREDIENTS

2 teaspoons butter lime juice

⅓ cup milk

½ cup butter, softened

¾ cup white sugar

1 egg

2 teaspoons lime zest

1¾ cups all-purpose flour

1 teaspoon baking powder

¼ teaspoon baking soda

2 teaspoons lime juice

¼ cup white sugar

DIRECTIONS

Preheat oven to 350 degrees.

Combine the 2 teaspoons of lime juice with the milk; let stand for 5 minutes.

In a large bowl, cream together the butter and ¾ cup sugar until light and fluffy. Beat in the egg, and then stir in the lime zest and milk mixture. Combine the flour, baking powder, and baking soda. Blend into the creamed mixture.

Drop by rounded spoonfuls onto the ungreased cookie sheets.

Bake for 8 to 10 minute in the preheated oven, until the edges are light brown.

Allow cookies to cool on baking sheets for 5 minutes before transferring to a wire rack to cool completely.

 **Mark T. Carboni** To get more juice from a lime, place it in a microwave for 15 seconds.

BALSAMIC PEACHES

Fresh peaches just found another great recipe!

INGREDIENTS

¾ **cup** balsamic vinegar

1 vanilla bean, split and seeds removed

4 donut peaches, pits removed and peels on

1 cup crème fraiche or plain yogurt

Mint sprigs (optional)

DIRECTIONS

In a large bowl, combine vinegar, scraped vanilla bean, and vanilla seeds. Mix with a whisk.

Add donut peaches and toss to coat with marinade. Marinate peaches for 2 hours or more, if desired. Turn every once in awhile to cover evenly.

To serve, remove peaches from vinegar and fill hole with a scoop of crème fraiche. Garnish with mint sprigs, if desired.

PRALINES – FRESH FROM YOUR MICROWAVE

Ever been to New Orleans? If you have, you will find this recipe to be very close to the pralines found on the square. If you have not, or have not tried a praline, then you really must live on the wild side and make this recipe.

INGREDIENTS

1 cup brown sugar

1 cup white sugar

¼ cup corn syrup

¼ cup water

1-2 tablespoon butter

1½ cup pecan halves

1 teaspoon vanilla

DIRECTIONS

In a microwavable bowl, place your sugars, syrup, water, and butter. Microwave on high heat for 4 minutes.

Remove, stir, and add the pecan halves and the vanilla. Microwave for another minute.

If the mixture does not show signs of sugar crystals, then stir the mixture for at least one minute continually. Let set for 30 seconds, stir again, and then dip out onto a cookie pan that has a wax paper lining. It should be about the size of a quarter, but there is nothing wrong with it being the size of a PLANKO chip. :-)

Refrigerate for an hour and then remove from the wax paper. You can keep these in a sealed container for about a week.

Mark T. Carboni Did your brown sugar harden on you? Add an apple and close. In a day, your brown sugar can be fluffed and used.

BROWNIE DIP

Always trying to determine what to make for dessert? I have found that dips are a great way to have a dessert ready in just minutes without much hassle.

INGREDIENTS

8 ounces cream cheese, light or regular, softened

¼ cup (4 tablespoons) butter, softened

2 cups powdered sugar

5 tablespoons all-purpose flour

5 tablespoons cocoa powder, regular or Dutch-process

2 tablespoons brown sugar

1 teaspoon vanilla

2-4 tablespoons milk

DIRECTIONS

Using an electric mixer, whip the cream cheese and butter together until light and fluffy, about 1-2 minutes.

Add the powdered sugar and mix well.

Add the flour, cocoa powder, brown sugar, vanilla, and 2 tablespoons milk. Mix until smooth.

Add additional powdered sugar or milk if needed, until the desired consistency is reached.

 **Melissa Fulmer** Hey Carbo, I'm going to the State Fair next Monday. Any must try food?

 **Mark T. Carboni** Beverage of choice: bubble tea. Main course: toss up between the cheese toasty at the Dairy Barn or the pork chop sandwich. The dessert would be deep fried brownies.

S'MORE PUDDING

No need to get the logs stacked outside, I have a s'more delight that will save you time and you won't smell like smoke (unless you catch your house on fire).

INGREDIENTS

4 cups miniature marshmallows

1¼ cups milk

10½ honey graham crackers, divided

1 (8 ounce) tub whipped topping, thawed

3 squares semi-sweet chocolate, divided

1 (8 ounce) package cream cheese, softened

1 (3.9 ounce) package chocolate instant pudding

½ cup fresh raspberries

DIRECTIONS

Microwave marshmallows and ¼ cup milk in a large microwaveable bowl for 90 seconds or until the marshmallows are completely melted, stirring after 1 minute. Stir until the mixture is well blended. Refrigerate for 10 minutes or until completely cooled.

Meanwhile, cover the bottom of a 9-inch square pan with half the grahams. Add 1 cup cool whip to the marshmallow mixture; whisk until well blended. Spread over the grahams in pan. Refrigerate until ready to use.

Melt 2 chocolate squares as directed on the package. Beat the cream cheese in a large bowl with a mixer until creamy. Gradually beat in the remaining milk. Add the dry pudding mix; beat for 2 minutes.

Whisk in the melted chocolate and 1 cup of the remaining cool whip; pour into the pan. Top with the remaining grahams. Refrigerate for 3 hours or until firm. Meanwhile, shave the remaining chocolate square into curls.

Invert the dessert onto a plate; remove the plastic wrap. Top the dessert with the remaining cool whip, berries, and chocolate curls.

 Dennis Meehan I've been asked to come up with a warm cocktail for a Christmas party this season. A company is having a Christmas luncheon here and I'm looking for hot, Christmas drinks. Any favorites?

 **Mark T. Carboni** This is not warm but feels warm: I call it S'mores & Cream.

2 parts Three Olives S'mores Vodka
4 parts Cream Soda

Marshmallow (toast it over a lighter and toss into your cocktail). Mix all ingredients together with ice and serve in a rocks glass. Garnish with a marshmallow!

 **Jim Clifton** I will spout off with one of my favorites too, hot chocolate and Malibu Rum (coconut flavor).

DESSERT CHIMICHANGA

What to do with those crazy bananas? Here you go, deep-fry them as a dessert!

INGREDIENTS

Nutella

1 banana

1 flour tortilla

Cinnamon-sugar mixture

DIRECTIONS

Spread Nutella to within 2 inches of the edge of the tortilla.

Place the banana in the tortilla. Roll up the tortilla. Seal the edges with water.

Deep fry until the tortilla is crispy and blistered.

Drain, then roll in the cinnamon-sugar.

Caryn Nave Okay, Mark T. Carboni, where's the martini recipe??? LOL

Mark T. Carboni A few years back I used to host an event called Martinis, Music and More where I introduced friends to new music along with eating and drinking along the way. This is my warm walnut martini that was a hit!

1-2 tablespoons heavy cream (or half and half to cut back on a few calories)
*1/2 ounce Nocino liqueur Walnut Liqueur
Dash of cinnamon
3 ounces espresso
1 ounce dark rum
Candied chestnut, walnut halves and whipped cream for garnish

In a cocktail shaker, combine the heavy cream, nocino liqueur, espresso and dark rum. Shake well. Pour into a martini glass and garnish with a candied chestnut, walnut halves and whipped cream. Serve immediately.

NUTELLA TRUFFLES

Looking for a way to make friends in the office? Package up a plate of the Nutella truffles and make an excuse to stop by desks with a treat.

INGREDIENTS

10 ounces favorite chocolate chip

2 tablespoons unsalted butter

½ cup heavy cream

½ cup Nutella

1 teaspoon vanilla extract

3 tablespoons chocolate vinegar

½ cup toasted hazelnuts, finely chopped

DIRECTIONS

In a double boiler over barely simmering water, combine chocolate, butter, heavy cream, and Nutella. Heat until chocolate is melted. Stir until you have a smooth mixture.

Remove the chocolate mixture from heat and allow it sit at room temperature for about 10 minutes. Whisk in vanilla and vinegar. Pour mixture into a shallow dish (e.g. 8 x 8 dish) and cover with plastic wrap. Refrigerate for about 2 hours. If you refrigerate longer than two hours, the mixture will be too hard to work with. If this occurs, allow the mixture to sit at room temperature until pliable enough to work with.

Line a baking sheet with parchment paper. Using a small scoop (2 teaspoons) or a melon baller, scoop out the chocolate mixture. Roll into one-inch balls and place on prepared baking sheet. Continue with remaining chocolate mixture. Roll the balls in chopped hazelnuts. Refrigerate truffles until ready to serve.

CHOCOLATE OVERLOAD CROCK POT CAKE

Who doesn't love a crockpot? The question may be better asked, who is tired of making the same things in your crockpot? Have you made a cake in one?

INGREDIENTS

1 (18 ounce) package chocolate cake mix

4 ounces cream cheese

1 cup water

¾ cup vegetable oil

4 eggs

8 ounces sour cream

1 (4 ounce) package instant chocolate pudding mix

4 ounces Nutella

DIRECTIONS

Spray a 4-quart crockpot with non-stick cooking spray and set aside.

In a large bowl, combine the cake mix and pudding mix.

In a medium bowl, beat the eggs with the water, then add the sour cream, cream cheese, Nutella, and oil. Beat until smooth. Add to the dry ingredients and beat well.

Pour into the crockpot. Cover and cook on low for 6-8 hours or until top springs back when touched very lightly. Makes 8-10 servings.

Mark T. Carboni Sour cream will last longer if you flip it upside down in the refrigerator and I always spray my crock pot with a non stick spray before cooking; makes cleaning easier.

PEANUT BUTTER BALLS

My grandmother used to make peanut butter balls and roll them in coconut. As a kid, I was fascinated. Now, I am just addicted.

INGREDIENTS

1 cup peanut butter

1 cup dry milk powder

½ cup honey

DIRECTIONS

Blend all ingredients together (preferably with hands). Roll into balls the size of large marbles and refrigerate. Optional: roll balls in powdered cocoa, or roll balls info flaked coconut, or dip into chocolate fondue. Eat and enjoy!

 **Mark T. Carboni** When measuring a sticky liquid, like honey, spray the measuring cup with a non-stick spray. Or just lick it clean if you really like honey.

CHRISTMAS CINNAMON ROLLS

There is something warm about a tradition to begin the holiday season. These Christmas cinnamon rolls may be a part of your holidays from today until the end of time:

INGREDIENTS

Rolls:

1 (¼ **ounce**) **package** dry yeast

1 **cup** warm milk

½ **cup** granulated sugar

⅓ **cup** margarine

1 **teaspoon** salt

2 eggs

4 **cups** flour

Filling:

1 **cup** packed brown sugar

3 **tablespoons** cinnamon

⅓ **cup** margarine, softened

3 **tablespoons** almond paste

Icing:

8 **tablespoons** margarine

1½ **cups** powdered sugar

¼ **cup cream** cheese

½ **teaspoon** vanilla

⅛ **teaspoon** salt

DIRECTIONS

For the rolls: in a large bowl, dissolve the yeast in the warm milk. Add sugar, margarine salt, eggs, and flour. Mix well. Knead the dough into a large ball, using your hands dusted lightly with flour. Put in a bowl, cover, and let rise in a warm place for about 1 hour or until the dough has doubled in size.

Roll the dough out on a lightly floured surface, until it is approximately 21 inches long by 16 inches wide. It should be approx ¼ inch thick. Preheat oven to 400 degrees.

To make the filling, combine the brown sugar, almond paste and cinnamon in a bowl. Spread the softened margarine over the surface of the dough, then sprinkle the brown sugar and cinnamon evenly over the surface. Working carefully, from the long edge, roll the dough down to the bottom edge. Cut the dough into 1¾ inch slices, and place in a lightly greased baking pan. Bake for 10 minutes or until light golden brown.

While the rolls are baking, combine the icing ingredients. Beat well with an electric mixer until fluffy.

When the rolls are done, spread generously with icing.

Mark T. Carboni Just the smell of cinnamon makes me feel hungry and create memories. Memories for anyone else?

Robb E. Maurer Absolutely. Christmas morning before packages are opened or thank yous are exchanged, my best friend and I get up and make our now infamous "Christmas Morning Cinnamon Rolls." This tradition is one that came about totally unexpectedly. We just wanted a morning treat to kick off the Christmas spirit of the day. I was given this recipe as a suggestion. My best friend's mother enjoyed seeing us goofy guys get up Christmas morning and play in the kitchen before anything else. Always a smile was across her face when she saw the finished product. Now that she is no longer with us, our Christmas morning tradition will continue on. I was but a stranger to her and she lovingly accepted me in as a part of her family. So for us, it is not simply baking cinnamon rolls on Christmas morning. You see, it is Christmas morning with Glenna "Mom" Schill. Thank you for the wonderful tradition you brought to our little family, Mr. Carboni!

ROOT BEER FLOAT ICE CREAM!

INGREDIENTS

8 ounces heavy cream

¼ cup brown sugar

8 ounces vanilla curd (jar)

8-12 ounce can root beer

DIRECTIONS

In a mixer, put in heavy cream and blend for a minute. Add the brown sugar and blend for 30 seconds. Add the vanilla curd and blend for 30 more seconds. Finally, add the root beer and blend for 1 minute.

Pour into a freezable bowl or pan. Let the ice cream harden for at least 4 hours.

 **Tracy Murray Mayer** I really want to make this. But what the heck is vanilla curd?

 **Mark T. Carboni** It's usually a dairy product made of curdling milk and adding ingredients such as eggs, butter, sugar and of course vanilla for vanilla curd. You can always try a recipe of your own but I usually use Dickinson's Vanilla Crème Curd found in a jar in the cooking aisle at the grocery store.

NO BAKE CAKE BATTER TRUFFLES

INGREDIENTS

½ **cup** unsalted butter, softened

¼ **cup** sugar

1½ **cups** flour

1 **cup** yellow cake mix, dry

1 **teaspoon** vanilla

⅛ **teaspoon** salt

2 **tablespoons** sprinkles

16 **ounces** white dipping chocolate

4 **tablespoons** yellow cake mix, dry

DIRECTIONS

Using an electric mixer, beat together the butter and sugar until combined.
Blend in vanilla. Add cake mix, flour, salt, and vanilla. Mix thoroughly.
Add 3 tablespoons of milk or more, if needed, to make a dough consistency.
Mix in sprinkles by hand. Roll dough into one inch balls and place on a
parchment or wax paper lined cookie sheet. Chill balls in the refrigerator for
15 minutes to firm up.

While dough balls are chilling, melt almond bark in the microwave in 30 second
intervals until melted. Stir between intervals. Once melted, quickly stir in cake
mix until incorporated completely. Using a fork, dip truffles into almond bark,
and shake off excess bark by tapping the bottom of the fork on the side of your
bowl. Place the truffle back on the cookie sheet and top with sprinkles. Repeat
with the remaining balls until finished.
(Note: for smoother looking truffles, don't add the cake mix to melted chocolate,
just leave it by itself.)

Chill cake batter truffles in the refrigerator until serving. Makes around
24-30 truffles.

Mark T. Carboni When you remove a cake from the oven and cool it on a rack. Place a slice of bread on top to draw away moisture. Reduces crumbs in the frosting.

CHOCOLATE PARSNIP PUDDING

INGREDIENTS

4 cups parsnips, peeled and chopped

1 cup almond milk

2 cups water

¼ **cup** sugar

1 teaspoon kosher salt

¼ **cup** cocoa powder

2 tablespoons butter

1 teaspoon almond extract

1 teaspoon cinnamon

DIRECTIONS

In a pot, bring to a boil the milk, water, parsnips, and half of the sugar. Once it comes to a boil, reduce the heat and allow to simmer for about 10 minutes, until parsnips are tender.

Drain the parsnips, reserving a cup of the cooking liquid for later use.

In a blender, place parsnips and remaining ingredients. Puree until smooth. If the mixture is not smooth, add some of the reserved liquid a little at a time.

Garnish with a mint leaf, basil, or edible flower

 **Mark T. Carboni** Parsnips: 1 pound parsnips = 4 servings.
1 pound = 3 cups chopped parsnips.
1 pound = 2 cups chopped, cooked parsnips.
1 pound = 4 to 6 small parsnips.

Parsnips may be substituted for carrots in most recipes
and vice versa.
They are very easy to cook with, actually, some people
enjoy roasting them in the oven.

I love almond milk and love that you can add it to most
recipes, just not good to bring it to a roaring boil or it will
taste bitter. Probably better to cook with or bake with
actually. On a stove, don't let it get up to 140 degrees.

INTRO TO APPETIZERS

 **Mark T. Carboni** If you could be in the kitchen with a celebrity, who would you want to cook with?

 **Liz Berry Schatzlein** Jon Stewart

 **Mitzi Adams** Anthony Bourdain

 **Lisa Thompson** Seriously...Giada. Love Italian and she seems fun.

 Jane Broemmelsiek Terrell Curtis Stone

 **Tim Jones** Betty White

 **JeanAnne Bailey** Robert Irvine

 **Jason Horn** I am pretty sure if you asked him, he would list me.

 **Mark T. Carboni** Jason, I was just about to say I bet Robert Irvine would like me in his kitchen and perhaps Betty White. But I would pick you too and share your amazing barbeque recipe.

 **Vicki Wells** Mark Carboni!

GOAT CHEESE MEDALLIONS

This is a great appetizer to start a party. The taste of goat cheese is one of those acquired tastes, but trust me, when you coat it and fry it, you will find this to be one acquisition of flavor you will hold near and dear.

INGREDIENTS

12 ounces goat cheese, separated into 1 ounce balls

4 eggs

½ cup half and half

2 cups all-purpose flour

4 cups herb crust, recipe follows

Salt and pepper, to taste

Crust:

½ bunch Italian parsley

¼ bunch sage (1 ounce)

¼ bunch thyme (1 ounce)

¼ bunch rosemary (1 ounce)

2 garlic cloves, minced

½ quart panko bread crumbs

1 ounce olive oil

DIRECTIONS

Form cheese balls into 1¼ inch diameter disks.

In a bowl, combine the eggs and half and half together. Place flour and herb crust into separate pans. Dredge cheese balls in the flour, then the egg mixture, and finally the herb crust.

Stack the medallions on parchment paper to prevent condensation. Fry the goat cheese medallions until golden brown. Drain.

 **Annette Bowen** Wonder if you have tried baking the goat cheese medallions instead of frying?

 **Mark T. Carboni** I have never baked them before but what a fabulous idea to make them healthier. Try them at 450 degree oven for 10 minutes and watch them closely.

A quick tip about those hard to slice cheeses: Warm your knife. It will cut like butter.

CHEESE TWIST STICKS

Tired of stale ole crackers? Who isn't? You can whip up a great dipstick without having to get your hands all oily. Ha! Anyway, this is a great party starter for any occasion.

INGREDIENTS

1 puff pastry – thawed and at room temperature for 30 minutes

1 large egg

½ cup Parmesan cheese, grated

Cracked pepper

DIRECTIONS

Beat one egg with one tablespoon of water.

Unfold the puff pastry and roll on a floured counter or board. With a pastry brush, use the egg mixture and brush it on. Sprinkle the cheese and the cracked pepper atop it. Fold the dough over and roll a few times to seal it.

Cut into ½ inch or 1 inch strips and twist.

Place in the oven at 400 degrees for 12 minutes.

 **Tim Jones** Sweet dreams are made of cheese, who am I to diss a Brie. I cheddar the world and the feta cheese, everybody's looking for Stilton.

 **Mark T. Carboni** Now that's a song I can sing.

ROSEMARY ALMONDS

Snacks will be brought to a new level with my rosemary almonds. Make a batch and they will serve two purposes: tasty snacks and kitchen air freshener.

INGREDIENTS

2 tablespoons butter

1 clove garlic, minced

1 tablespoon rosemary, minced

1½ cup whole almonds

Salt

2 tablespoons Worcestershire sauce

DIRECTIONS

Melt the butter in a large skillet. Add the garlic and rosemary. When the garlic has changed colors, add the almonds. Stir. Add the salt and the Worcestershire sauce.

Once all the almonds have been glazed with the liquids, place on a sheet pan in the oven at 350 degrees for 8 minutes.

Mark T. Carboni Anyone have trouble getting the skin off of a clove of garlic? Just zap it in the microwave for 15 seconds and voila!

ASPARAGUS TWIST STICKS

This may be the only time when hiding your vegetables on the plate is not only acceptable, but desired. Give these asparagus twists a twirl.

INGREDIENTS

1 puff pastry – thawed and at room temperature for 30 minutes

1 large egg

½ cup Parmesan cheese, grated

12 asparagus spears

Cracked pepper

DIRECTIONS

Beat one egg with one tablespoon water.

Unfold the puff pastry and roll on a floured counter or board. With a pastry brush, use the egg mixture and brush it on. Cut into 1 inch strips. Sprinkle the cheese and the cracked pepper atop it.

Wrap the dough around the asparagus.

Place in oven at 400 degrees for 12 minutes.

 **Jory Katras Stiffarm** Carbo – what would we do without cheese? Gives me shivers to think about it.

 **Mark T. Carboni** Trust me I know... it is its own food group, LOL.

If you are grating that cheese yourself just give your grater a quick spay with a non-stick spray; makes cleaning a whole lot easier.

SPICY WHITE BEAN AND AVOCADO

Sometimes we find ourselves with very ripe avocados. This will be a great recipe to not only use them up, but also actually aspire to have avocados expire so you can make this dip.

INGREDIENTS

2 ripe avocados, peeled and pitted

1 can northern beans

2 garlic cloves, minced

½ or 1 jalapeno (depending if you like heat)

¼ cup chopped cilantro

¼ cup chopped mint

2 teaspoon lime juice

1 teaspoon extra virgin olive oil

1 teaspoon salt

1 teaspoon pepper

DIRECTIONS

Place the avocados, beans, garlic, and jalapeno in a bowl and mash with a fork. Add the remainder of the items and mix together.

 **Mark T. Carboni** Bacon hard to separate in the packaging sleeve? Roll if first before opening for easy bacon separation.

 **Linda Cambre** Thanks, Mark. One of my favorite ways to keep the bacon from curling when cooking is to soak in cold water beforehand. It really makes a difference.

 **Mark T. Carboni** Thanks, Linda, that's a great idea, especially when you are trying to make sandwiches. That's tough with curled up bacon.

CHORIZO DIP

Carbo loves to host a party. I also love a great dip that packs some heat and yet makes you come back for more. Grab your tortilla chips!

INGREDIENTS

1 pound chorizo

1 onion, diced

1 jalapeño, diced

1 cup salsa

½ package tex mex shredded cheese

1 package cream cheese

2 tablespoons cilantro

3 tablespoons milk

DIRECTIONS

Remove the sausage meat from its casing and brown in a large fry pan. Add the onion and sauté until translucent. Add the jalapeño, salsa, and tequila, and mix well. Simmer.

Dice the cream cheese into large chunks and add to the fry pan, stirring to melt. Add the tex mex cheese and melt, stirring. Loosen up the dip with 3 tablespoons milk. Add the cilantro. Transfer to a warm cast iron pan. At this point you can refrigerate until ready to serve.

Reheat in a 325 degree oven for 20 minutes or until heated through.

Garnish with cheese, tomato, and cilantro if desired, and serve with tortilla chips.

 **Mark T. Carboni** Ever need buttermilk for a recipe and all you have on hand is milk in the refrigerator? Just add 1 tablespoon of lemon juice to a cup of milk and you have your Buttermilk substitute.

ZUCCHINI CHIPS

When it comes to harvesting your personal garden, you will find zucchini grows plentiful and rapidly. This is a great way to enjoy them besides a loaf of zucchini bread.

INGREDIENTS

¼ **cup** dry bread crumbs

¼ **cup (1 ounce)** grated fresh Parmesan cheese

¼ **teaspoon** seasoned salt

¼ **teaspoon** garlic powder

⅛ **teaspoon** freshly ground black pepper

2 **tablespoons** milk

2½ **cups (¼ inch thick) slices** zucchini (about 2 small)

Cooking spray

DIRECTIONS

Preheat oven to 425 degrees.

Combine first 5 ingredients in a medium bowl, stirring with a whisk. Place milk in a shallow bowl. Dip zucchini slices in milk, and dredge in bread crumb mixture.

Place coated slices on an ovenproof wire rack coated with cooking spray; place rack on a baking sheet.

Bake at 425 degrees for 30 minutes, or until brown and crisp.

Serve immediately.

 **Mark T. Carboni** Another great way to use your cooking spray, spritz some on top of your guacamole and it will help keep your fabulous dip green.

BLACK BEAN AND JALAPENO DIP

I have always found the black bean to be an interesting bean, but I never know when to use it. This was one way I have found to make it a kick-off to a perfect dinner.

INGREDIENTS

1 can black beans, drained

1 can diced tomatoes, drained

1 jalapenos, chopped

1 lime,juiced

1 tablespoon heavy cream

1 teaspoon coriander

Salt

DIRECTIONS

First of all, drain the black beans and rinse them under cold running water. Now, place half of them in the goblet of a food processor, and then add the tomatoes, jalapeno peppers, lime juice, and coriander. Season well with some salt and whiz the whole lot until it is quite smooth.

Next, add the rest of the black beans and give these a short burst in the processor (this is to give the dip a little bit of texture). Now transfer it all to a bowl and fold in the cream.

Taste to check the seasoning, and then serve garnished with some more coriander and wedges of lime.

Use potato wedges (or whatever else you fancy) to dip with.

Mark T. Carboni To ripen a tomato, place in a paper bag along with an apple.

PULL APART PIZZA BREAD

Fun in the kitchen begins with this recipe. It is a great recipe to get the kids involved.

INGREDIENTS

8 ounces sliced mushrooms

1 tablespoon butter

2 cloves garlic, minced

½ pound ground sausage

8 ounces tomato sauce

1 unsliced loaf sourdough bread

12 ounces mozzarella cheese shredded

½ cup butter, melted

DIRECTIONS

Heat a medium-sized skillet on medium heat. Add the butter. Once the butter is melted, add the mushrooms and garlic. Cook 4-5 minutes until they start to sweat. Add the sausage and tomato sauce. Mix well. Set aside and allow to cool.

Preheat oven to 350 degrees.

Cut the bread lengthwise and widthwise without cutting through the bottom crust. This can be a little tricky going the second way, but the bread is very forgiving.

Place the loaf on a foil-lined baking sheet. Insert the cheese slices between cuts. Pour the mushrooms/sausage between the cuts. Use your fingers to push the mixture down into the loaf. Pour the melted butter over the top of the bread.

Bake at 350 degrees for 15 minutes. Unwrap the bread and bake for 10 more minutes, or until the cheese is melted.

 **Mark T. Carboni** To avoid butter splattering in a microwave, place a saucer of water in at the same time.

BUFFALO CHICKEN DIP

Think Super Bowl. Now think Empty Bowl, because it will be when you put this appetizer in front of a huddle of people.

INGREDIENTS

8 ounces cream cheese

½ cup finely chopped celery

½ cup hot sauce (recommended: Frank's)

1 rotisserie chicken, shredded

1 cup crumbled bleu cheese

Crackers, bread or carrot sticks, for serving.

DIRECTIONS

Preheat the oven to 425 degrees.

In a medium saucepan over moderate heat, melt the cream cheese until smooth, about 3 minutes. Add the celery, hot sauce, and chicken. Mix well.

Transfer the mixture to a 9-inch pie plate and sprinkle the crumbled bleu cheese on top. Bake until hot and bubbly, about 25 minutes.

Serve with crackers, bread, or carrot sticks.

 Marcus Method Jr Do you have a recipe for good buffalo chicken dip and also a good bleu cheese filled dip?

 **Mark T. Carboni** This is a great and quick blue cheese dip:

4 ounce bleu cheese
1/4 cup mayonnaise
1/4 cup sour cream
1 tablespoon chopped chives

Mix all ingredients in a bowl and serve with crackers or vegetables.

CARBO'S PINEAPPLE AND SHRIMP COCKTAIL

Celebrating with friends and family should be fun and relaxing. Making a dinner or a pre-dinner starter can be stressful when time and joy of cooking is not bountiful. This is a recipe you can make with ease. The colors are rich and the smell and taste are beyond words. When you have a group of 8 or less coming over, this recipe will be a perfect start to a wonderful evening.

INGREDIENTS

1 pound pre-cooked shrimp tails

1 cup pineapple juice

2 blood oranges, juiced

2 limes, juiced

1 cup pineapple diced

6 mint leaves

Salt/pepper

DIRECTIONS

Combine all ingredients, except mint, in a large bowl.

Refrigerate until ready to serve.

Place in margarita glasses. Garnish with shredded mint on top.

 **Mark T. Carboni** When picking out an orange, the best ones should be firm and heavy

WATERMELON DRIZZLE

Summer comes to life only when I see a lightening bug or taste the sweet taste of a watermelon. Until then, it is simply a hot day. Growing up, my godmother would pair ice cream with fresh cut watermelon as my treat every time I saw her. Later in my life, I wondered about combining the textures to make a more sophisticated appetizer. This recipe can be made for as many people as you want. Simply, it is equal parts of the ingredients held together by the magic of a toothpick.

INGREDIENTS

Watermelon

Mint leaves

Goat cheese

Balsamic vinegar

DIRECTIONS

Dice watermelon into inch by inch squares. Add a fresh mint leaf onto each square of watermelon. Roll goat cheese into half-inch circles, add on top of mint leaf and watermelon. Drizzle with your favorite balsamic vinegar. Spear with a tooth pick and serve.

 **Mark T. Carboni** Not a fan of vinegar? Substitute grapefruit juice.

CARBO'S SALSA

When Carbo has a gathering of friends, he is always on the search for the perfect opening bites of food, and a comfortable surrounding. Bring your friends together around a bowl of homemade salsa that is painfully simple and tasty! Whether it is a Memorial Day picnic or a book club night, you will find this salsa to be a hit!

INGREDIENTS

3 roma tomatoes

3 kumato tomatoes

1 anheim pepper

1 medium onion

4 cloves garlic

1 bunch cilantro

Cayenne olive oil

1 tablespoon Olive Twist organic lime olive oil

¼ teaspoon Olive Twist spicy hot red

1 tablespoon Olive Twist honey ginger white balsamic vinegar

2 limes

1 teaspoon salt

DIRECTIONS

Dice 2 roma and kumato tomatoes, the pepper, onion, and cilantro. Mince the garlic, and then add to the tomato mixture. Juice two limes and add to the tomato mixture.

In a blender, place one roma and kumato tomato, the lime oil, the cayenne oil, and the honey ginger, and blend until smooth.

Add the liquid mixture to the tomato mixture. Add the salt and stir.

Refrigerate at least one half hour to infuse the flavors.

This party favorite will be a great appetizer for up to 8 people.

Mark T. Carboni Save extra green onions in the freezer in a plastic water bottle. It will keep them fresher longer.

BACON AVOCADO DIP: EVEN GUACAMOLE LOVES BACON

HUGE and exciting news! One of our Cookin' with Carbo recipes has made it into a Bandidos restaurant for its seasonal menu.

INGREDIENTS

3 ripe avocados

1 clove garlic, minced

1 small lime, juiced

6 slices bacon, cooked and diced

3 tablespoons fresh chopped cilantro

Salt and pepper to taste

DIRECTIONS

Scoop the avocado from the shells and place in a large bowl. Add garlic, lime, salt, and pepper. With the back of a wooden spoon, smash the avocado against the bowl. It should be somewhat chunky. Mix in a circular motion to incorporate all the ingredients. Drop in the bacon and cilantro and mix again.

Serve within an hour of making for best flavors.

GRILLED MEATBALLS

Time to create some fabulous meatballs for your guests, or have them create a spice mix or dip of their own. Here are two suggestions from my facebook friends, but first, a quick grilled meatball recipe to get you started.

INGREDIENTS

2 pounds ground beef

2 eggs, lightly beaten

½ teaspoon salt

DIRECTIONS

In a bowl, combine the beef, eggs, and ½ teaspoon salt. Mix until mixture holds together well. Form into twelve 3-inch balls and thread them onto metal skewers to place on the grill or under the broiler in your oven.

Brush the meatballs with olive oil and sprinkle with seasoning mix or plum bourbon BBQ sauce (recipe to follow). Place the skewers on an oiled grill rack or broiler pan. Cook until brown on all sides and cooked through, about 8-10 minutes.

Slide the meatballs off the skewers and serve.

PLUM BOURBON BBQ SAUCE FROM JASON HORN

INGREDIENTS

2 pounds plums, halved and pitted

8 ounces chopped onion
(about 1.5 medium)

1-2 jalapenos, halved
(depends on heat tolerance)

1 clove garlic

1 tablespoon chopped ginger

1 cup brown sugar

½ cup cider vinegar

¼ cup bourbon

¼ cup honey

¼ cup ketchup

2 tablespoons molasses

1 tablespoon worcestershire sauce

1 tablespoon dijon mustard,
whole grain or smooth

1 teaspoon kosher salt

DIRECTIONS

Combine all ingredients in a large pot. My enamel dutch oven was deep enough to catch the lava-like sputters, and the wide mouth ensured fast evaporation, great for thickening the sauce. Bring to a boil and reduce to a simmer. When the fruit seems soft enough to mash, after about 10 minutes of simmering, use an immersion blender to puree.

Let simmer for 30 minutes, stirring occasionally to avoid scorching. Take a spoonful of sauce and let it cool on a plate. Taste it. How do you feel about it? If the flavors seem a bit off, play a bit with additional amounts of the ingredient list. If it's too runny, keep simmering; too thick, add some bourbon, stock, or water. Keep in mind; the sauce will thicken as it cools.

Once you're happy with the flavor and consistency, chill out. Let the sauce cool for 10 minutes, and bottle or jar it in the containers of choice. Let the containers cool completely and refrigerate.

Great to toss onto some cooked meatballs that will just soak up the flavor.

This party favorite will be a great appetizer for up to 8 people.

Jason Horn is The Dive Whisperer and travels, city by city, and introduces you to the fine compatriots of the local dive bars, their signature drinks, and signature dishes. Expect to learn a few bar tricks, meet fascinating people, and learn where the best bar food is! www.thedivewhisper.com

SPICE GRILLED BURGER BITES FROM BILL WEST

INGREDIENTS

½ **teaspoon** ancho chile

½ **teaspoon** onion powder

1 **teaspoon** marjoram

1 **teaspoon** garlic

1 **teaspoon** oregano

1 **teaspoon** cayenne pepper

1 **teaspoon** cinnamon

1 **teaspoon** coriander

1 **teaspoon** ginger

½ **teaspoon** freshly ground black pepper

½ **teaspoon** salt

Olive oil for brushing

DIRECTIONS

Combine the onions, parsley, coriander, and turmeric. Toss well and set aside.

Preheat the grill or broiler.

It's best to brush the meatballs with olive oil before sprinkling with seasoning mix, so the spices adhere and give the burger bites tenderness.

INTRO TO SOUPS

 **Mark T. Carboni** With everyone having great chili recipes, what are your favorite ingredients to add?

 **Lisa Underwood** My husband Chris makes the best chili. Red kidney beans, V8 juice, hamburger (grilled on the gas grill first for that outdoor taste), onions and lots of different seasonings. Topped with cheddar cheese in the bowl. YUM.

 **Melissa Rasner** I like to do the traditional but add hot sauce, hot peppers, and hot chili beans. I serve it with sour cream, extra hot sauce, crackers on the side and of course shredded cheddar. And it goes great with pb&j sandwiches!

 **Jennifer Green Showalter** Chicken, cumin and cilantro.

 **Janie Ebinger** Lots of habaneros and pinto beans.

 **Melissa Killen** Ground elk burger, black beans, red beans and chili beans, tomato sauce and tomatoes, seasonings and lots of corn bread.

 **Jane Trueblood** Lots of meat, kidney beans, black beans, tomato paste, beef stock, a little cayenne pepper, a little onion, etc. Sounds so good right now!

 **Mary Mort** Black beans, blackeyed peas, bushes baked beans, 85, angus beef, diced tomatoes, my homemade meat balls, tomato paste, tomato sauce, chilli powder and my secret molasses.

 **Theresa Compton** It is best Cincinnati-style, served on top of spaghetti, with lots of cheese!

TUSCAN SOUP

A tradition I had with my mother when she would return from Florida was a trip to the Olive Garden. I would have the tuscan soup every time, and we always joked about how each bowl was different in content, just as every chef has their own style. Try my version of this tuscan soup.

INGREDIENTS

1 pound italian sausage, cooked and crumbled

1 pound bacon, cooked and crumbled

5 medium russet potatoes, sliced thin

2 cups kale, chopped

1 cup heavy whipping cream

48 ounces chicken broth

1 bag chopped onions (frozen)

3 cloves garlic, minced

2 teaspoons red pepper flakes

Salt and pepper

DIRECTIONS

In a pot, place potatoes, onion, garlic, and chicken broth on medium heat until the potatoes are cooked through.

Prepare the kale by chopping into bite-sized pieces.

Add the sausage, bacon, red pepper flakes, and salt and pepper to taste.

Simmer for another 10 minutes, stirring occasionally. Turn the heat to low and add in the kale and heavy cream.

 **Terry Lunde** Hi, I have 2 large left over baked potatoes. Any good ideas on how to use them?

 **Mark T. Carboni** I would consider making a soup. Consider dicing the potatoes, adding 4 cups of chicken broth and bring to a boil. Turn down the heat and add a pound of diced shrimp and a cup of frozen corn. You can add sauteed onions, pepper and celery. Add a tablespoon of flour to the mixture before you put it into the broth. Turn the heat down and add a cup of cream and diced bacon (about a half pound). On medium heat cook for about 2–3 minutes. Salt and pepper to taste. A quick potato corn and shrimp soup.

BUFFALO CHICKEN SOUP

When winter rolls around, I find that I can't get enough soup. This is a soup that will give you something to remember the next day.

INGREDIENTS

2 boneless, skinless chicken breasts, cooked and shredded

2 tablespoons olive oil

½ **bag** frozen onions

2 cloves garlic, minced

1 tablespoon flour

32 ounces chicken broth

⅓-½ **cup** buffalo wing sauce

⅓ **cup** cheddar cheese, freshly grated

¼ **cup** Parmesan cheese, freshly grated

DIRECTIONS

Heat a large pot over medium heat and add olive oil.

Add onions with a sprinkle of salt to the pot, stirring to coat, then cook for about 5 minutes until soft. Add in garlic and cook for 1-2 minutes more. Sprinkle in flour and stir for another 1-2 minutes. Add in chicken broth, buffalo sauce, chicken, and grated cheeses, stirring constantly.

Bring to a boil, then reduce and let simmer for 10-15 minutes, stirring every so often.

 Mark T. Carboni When mincing garlic, sprinkle on a little salt so the pieces won't stick to your knife or cutting board.

WHITE BEAN CILANTRO LIME SOUP

Fan favorite! At our Cookin' with Carbo cooking classes, this was a highlight of the day. Nearly everyone found this remarkably wonderful and one their favorites.

INGREDIENTS

3 cans northern beans

2 limes (juice and zest)

3 cloves garlic, minced

3 tablespoons extra virgin olive oil

2 cups vegetable (or chicken) stock

⅓ cup onion, chopped

A good handful of cilantro, chopped

Salt and pepper to taste

DIRECTIONS

In a stockpot, combine the oil, onion, and garlic. When onions and garlic cook down a bit, add the beans and lime zest. Cook for another minute or two.

Add in the chicken broth. Then, add the cilantro and lime juice. Cover with a lid and bring to a slight boil. Reduce heat to low and simmer for another 5 minutes.

Cool long enough to blend and to make the soup very smooth.

Add a bit of salt and pepper to taste, if needed. Set aside with the lid on tight to keep the soup hot while you finish making any other sides.

CAJUN CORN AND SHRIMP SOUP

One of our Cookin' with Carbo tours brought us to New Orleans.
This recipe will give you a first class ticket to the flavors found in the city
that never sleeps.

INGREDIENTS

½ **pound** pepper bacon, chopped

1 **cup** onion, chopped

½ **cup** celery, chopped

1 **teaspoon** fresh thyme, chopped

1 garlic clove, minced

4 **cups** fresh or frozen corn, thawed

2 **cups** chicken broth

¾ **pound** shimp, peeled, deveined, free of tails

⅓ **cup** heavy cream

¼ **teaspoon** black pepper

⅛ **teaspoon** salt

DIRECTIONS

Heat a large dutch oven over medium-high heat. Add the bacon to the pan.
Sauté for 4 minutes or until the bacon begins to brown. Remove 2 slices of
bacon. Drain on a paper towels. Add the onion and the next 3 ingredients
(through minced garlic) to pan, and sauté for 2 minutes. Add corn, and cook
for 2 minutes, stirring occasionally. Add the broth; bring to a boil, and cook
for 4 minutes.

Place 2 cups of corn mixture in a blender. Remove the centerpiece of the
blender lid (to allow steam to escape), and secure the lid on the blender.
Place a clean towel over the opening in the blender lid (to avoid splatters).
Blend until smooth. Return puréed corn mixture to pan. Stir in shrimp; cook
for 2 minutes or until the shrimp are done. Stir in the heavy cream, pepper,
and salt. Crumble the reserved bacon over the soup.

HOT AND SOUR SOUP

I have always found chinese food to be difficult to make at home. I tackled one of my favorite soups, and I believe you will love the ease and simplicity of this hot and sour soup.

INGREDIENTS

3 **cups** chicken broth

½ **cup** sliced mushrooms

1 **tablespoon** soy sauce

1 **(8 ounce) can** sliced bamboo shoots, drained

3 **tablespoons** fresh lemon juice

1 **teaspoon** white pepper

1½ **pounds** medium shrimp, peeled and deveined

8 **ounces** firm tofu, drained and cut into 1 inch cubes

1 **tablespoon** cornstarch

2 **tablespoons** water

1 large egg white, beaten

¼ **teaspoon** chili oil

2 **tablespoons** chopped green onions

DIRECTIONS

Combine the first 4 ingredients in a large saucepan; bring to a boil. Reduce heat and simmer for 5 minutes.

Add juice, pepper, shrimp, and tofu to pan; bring to a boil. Cook for 2 minutes or until the shrimp are almost done.

Combine the cornstarch and water in a small bowl, stirring until smooth. Add the cornstarch mixture to the pan. Cook for 1 minute, stirring constantly with a whisk. Slowly drizzle the egg white into the pan, stirring constantly.

Remove from heat; stir in the chili oil and onions.

 **Mark T. Carboni** Ever drop an egg on the floor while cooking? Sweeten it up! Yep, add sugar to make the clean up easier.

TACO SOUP

Making tacos has always been one of those time-eating tasks that never feels as if it pays off in the end. Try this taco soup for your taco fix.

INGREDIENTS

2 pounds ground beef

1 onion, chopped

2 cans baked beans

1 can whole kernel corn

1 can diced tomatoes with green chile peppers

1 can peeled and diced tomatoes with juice

1 (1.25 ounce) package taco seasoning mix

DIRECTIONS

In a large pot over medium high heat, combine the ground beef and onion, and sauté until the meat is browned and the onion is tender.

Add the beans, corn, tomatoes, green chile peppers, tomatoes, and taco seasoning. Mix well.

Reduce heat to medium and allow to heat through, about 15 minutes.

CHILLED PEACH SOUP

I think in a former life, I must have grown up in the south. I watch the Real Housewives of Atlanta and can only imagine the scent of peach cobbler mixed with a heavy dose of drama. Yum! Anyway, this soup brings out the best of my favorite piece of fruit.

INGREDIENTS

1 cup fresh or frozen raspberries, thawed

3 cups fresh or frozen peaches, thawed

3 tablespoon lemon juice

1 cup peach nectar

1 cup plain yogurt

¼ cup sugar

1 teaspoon almond extract

DIRECTIONS

Place the raspberries in a blender; cover and process until smooth. Strain and discard seeds. Cover and refrigerate puree.

Place the peaches and lemon juice in the blender; cover and process until smooth.

Transfer to a bowl; sit in nectar, yogurt, and sugar if needed (if fruit is tart), and extract. Cover and refrigerate for 2 hours.

MUSHROOM BRIE BISQUE

A quick soup packed with amazing flavor without having to pack a suitcase to Paris! N'est Pas? A rich, creamy, and filling soup. Perfect for a chilly fall evening.

INGREDIENTS

2 tablespoons butter

2 shallots, minced

6 portabella mushroom caps, cleaned and chopped

8 ounces white mushrooms, cleaned and chopped

6 cups chicken broth

2 cups heavy cream

8 ounces brie cheese, rind removed, cubed

2 tablespoons cornstarch

2 tablespoons water

DIRECTIONS

Heat the butter in a large saucepan over medium-high heat. Add the mushrooms and shallots, and sauté until most of the water has cooked out of the mushrooms, about 5 minutes. Add the chicken stock. Simmer for 15 minutes. Add the heavy cream as well as the chunks of brie cheese.

Simmer the soup, whisking until the cheese melts down. Make a "slurry" with the cornstarch and water, and whisk into the soup to thicken. Bring to a soft rolling boil and remove from heat. Season with salt and pepper to taste.

BRAZILIAN SHRIMP SOUP

I love to try foods from other nations. I once had a party of "Foods From Multi-Nations." What an array of flavors and spice combinations. I think we all need to challenge our taste buds from time to time.

INGREDIENTS

2 **tablespoons** cooking oil

1 onion, chopped

1 green bell pepper, chopped

3 **cloves** garlic, minced

¾ **cup** long-grain rice

¼ **teaspoons** red pepper flakes

1¾ **teaspoon** salt

1¾ **cups** canned crushed tomatoes in thick puree (from one 15 ounce can)

5 **cups** water

1 **cup** canned unsweetened coconut milk

1½ **pounds** medium shrimp, shelled and cut in half horizontally

¼ **teaspoon** fresh ground black pepper

1 **tablespoon** lemon juice

½ **cup** chopped fresh parsley or cilantro

DIRECTIONS

In a large pot, heat the oil over moderately low heat. Add the onion, bell pepper, and garlic. Cook, stirring occasionally, until the vegetables start to soften, about 10 minutes.

Add the rice, red-pepper flakes, salt, tomatoes, and water to the pot. Bring to a boil and cook until the rice is almost tender, about 10 minutes.

Stir the coconut milk into the soup. Bring back to a simmer and then stir in the shrimp. Simmer, stirring occasionally, until the shrimp are just done (3 to 5 minutes). Stir in the black pepper, lemon juice, and parsley.

Variation: instead of the shrimp, use one pound of boneless, skinless chicken breast (about three), cut crosswise into quarter-inch strips. Cook for the same amount of time.

CURRIED CAULIFLOWER SOUP

Growing up Carbo, cauliflower was not a word we heard often, let alone ate. I am uncertain why, other than it has always reminded me of a brain. Now that I have said that, as an adult I find that I do like it, and this soup is one example of a way to enjoy it.

INGREDIENTS

¼ **cup** raw sunflower kernels

1 **tablespoon** almond milk

1 **teaspoons** curry powder

1 **cup** yellow onion, chopped

3 **cloves** garlic, chopped

5 **cups (about 1 pound)** cauliflower florets, chopped

3 **teaspoons** curry powder

DIRECTIONS

Preheat oven to 350 degrees. In a medium bowl, toss sunflower kernels with 1 teaspoon almond milk and 1 teaspoon curry powder. Spread out on a small parchment paper lined baking sheet and bake. Toss once or twice, until toasted and fragrant. Bake 6 to 8 minutes; set aside.

On a sheet pan place the cauliflower, onion, and garlic. Drizzle with a garlic olive oil. Roast at 400 degrees for 20 minutes.

Working in batches, carefully purée the roasted vegetables in a blender and add the second portion of curry powder. Blend until smooth. Transfer to bowls and garnish with sunflower seeds.

CORN CHOWDER

Who says that vegetarian food has to be bland or only for vegetarians? This recipe will be added to your soup list of must-makes!

INGREDIENTS

2 **(12 ounce) bags** frozen corn

3 **cups** vegetable broth

2 large sweet potatoes, diced

1 large onion, diced

1 clove garlic, minced

2 red chile peppers, minced

1 tablespoon chili powder

2 teaspoons salt

1 tablespoon parsley flakes

Black pepper to taste

1¾ **cups** soy milk

¼ **cup** margarine

1 lime, juiced

DIRECTIONS

Place the corn, vegetable broth, potatoes, onion, garlic, red chile peppers, chili powder, salt, parsley, and black pepper in a slow cooker; cover. Cook on low for 7 hours.

Pour the vegetable mixture into a blender, filling the pitcher no more than halfway full. Hold the lid of the blender with a folded kitchen towel and carefully start the blender using a few quick pulses before leaving it on to purée. Purée in batches until smooth, and pour into a clean pot. Alternately, you can use a stick blender and purée the mixture in the cooking pot.

Once everything has been puréed, return it to the slow cooker. Stir the soy milk and margarine to the mixture; cook on low for 1 hour more. Add the lime juice to serve.

JAMBALAYA

People ask, "Carbo, what is your favorite meal?" Well, clocking in at the top three would be jambalaya!

INGREDIENTS

12-18 shrimp, free of tails

1 pound cooked chicken, diced

1 tablespoon creole seasoning

2 tablespoons olive oil

¼ cup onion, chopped

¼ cup green bell pepper, chopped

¼ cup celery, chopped

2 tablespoons chopped garlic

1 cup bloody mary mix

1 teaspoon Worcestershire sauce

1 teaspoon hot sauce

1 cup rice

3 cups chicken stock

1 pound andouille sausage, sliced

Salt and pepper

DIRECTIONS

In a bowl, combine the shrimp, chicken, and creole seasoning, and work in the seasoning well.

In a large saucepan, heat the oil over high heat with onion, pepper, and celery for 3 minutes. Add garlic, bloody mary mix, bay leaves, Worcestershire, and hot sauces. Stir in the rice and slowly add the broth. Reduce heat to medium and cook until the rice absorbs the liquid and becomes tender. Cook for about 15 minutes, stirring occasionally.

When the rice is just tender, add shrimp, chicken mixture, and sausage. Cook until the meat is done, about 10 minutes more. Season to taste with salt, pepper, and creole seasoning.

 **Mark T. Carboni** To make your white rice vibrant, add a squeeze of fresh lemon.

CANTALOUPE SOUP

It is like a spa, without the expensive price tag.

INGREDIENTS

1 cantaloupe, peeled, seeded and cubed

2 cups orange juice

1 tablespoon fresh lime juice

¼ teaspoon ground cinnamon

DIRECTIONS

Peel, seed, and cube the cantaloupe.

Place the cantaloupe and ½ cup orange juice in a blender or food processor. Cover, and process until smooth. Transfer to a large bowl. Stir in the lime juice, cinnamon, and remaining orange juice. Cover, and refrigerate for at least one hour.

Garnish with mint if desired.

Mark T. Carboni A cantaloupe is best when it does not have a strong smell. As it is with all melons, the heavier the better for its size (means there is a lot of juice). It's also best if the fruit is even in color and free of bruises.

SPICY PUMPKIN SOUP

When fall comes, I love to find a warm soup to cuddle up with and bask in the warm undertones that envelop. They can only be found in a thick, warm, and comforting soup.

INGREDIENTS

2 cloves garlic, minced

1 tablespoon olive oil

½ cup dry white wine

1 onion, diced

1 teaspoon sugar

2 cups vegetable or chicken broth

1 teaspoon nutmeg

1 tablespoon ground coriander

1 tablespoon fresh ginger, grated

Pinch cayenne pepper

1 teaspoon cinnamon

1 cup heavy cream

15 ounces canned pumpkin

DIRECTIONS

Heat the oil in a big pot and sauté the onions until golden brown.

Add the ginger and garlic. Sauté for about thirty seconds. Add the spices and cook until fragrant, without letting them burn. Add the wine and stir, cooking for another minute.

Remove the soup from the heat. Add the pumpkin and one cup of liquid, and purée with a food processor or stick blender.

When the soup is smooth, heat it in the pot with the remaining liquid until it reaches a simmer.

Add sugar, some raw grated ginger, or some salt, depending on the desired taste.

 **Jane Trueblood** I added wild rice before, with your pumpkin soup. The black and white grains in with the golden orange soup looked so pretty. It was delicious and it freezes/reheats very well too.

 **Mark T. Carboni** Great idea Jane, sounds like a gorgeous bowl of soup.

101

AFTERWARD

One.

Yes indeed, that seems to be the hardest number to invite to a dinner party. Perhaps that makes an odd number at the table or someone feels obligated to invite a potential "guest" for me. But not for Mark Carboni.

I spent 43 years being a single lady and when I met Mark he didn't care. He would make dinners and parties for a mix of people. They would be married, single, widowed, with children, without children and everything else in between. Friends of all backgrounds, ages, and marital statuses were brought together under one roof and friendships were created during these gatherings. Alone you didn't have to be with Mark as your friend. You see that is his gift.

I have enjoyed working on Mark's cookbook because I am happy to put a spotlight on his talents, his gift. Now I know in this world of social media, cell phones and more perhaps we interact even less face to face but that is why it's even more important to learn how to help people meet and make friends. Can food and cooking create friendships? Absolutely, and hopefully a few tips and insights in this book will make it sound even easier for you to try.

I think Three Dog Night had it wrong; one is not the loneliest number.

Sincerely,
Jessica Gize